This
Journal
BELONGS

To
↓

I LOVE

Everything That's old:

Old Friends,
Old Times,
Old manners,
Old Books,
Old Wines...

oliver
goldsmith

a Bottle
of
WINE
BEgS
TO BE
Shared...
clifton Fadiman

WINE

to me is passion. It's FAMILY and FRIENDS. It's warmth of HEART and generosity of SPIRIT. WINE IS ART. IT'S CULTURE. It's the ESSENCE of CIVILIZATION and THE ART of LIVING.

Robert Mondavi

WINE IS SUNLIGHT, held Together BY WatEr.

galileo galilei

WINE
maKES EVERY MEAL
an OccaSIoN,
EVERY TABLE MoRE
ELEGANT,
EVERY DAY MoRE
CIVILIZED.

andré SIMON

good WINE
is
a NECESSITY
of LIFE

FOR
ME. Thomas
JEFFErSON

ACCEPT
what LIFE
offers you And
TRY TO DRINK
FROM EVERY CUP,
ALL WINES
Should BE TasTed,
Some Should ONLY
BE SIPPEd,
But with others,
DRINK
The whole
BOTTLE.

Paulo CoElho

GENTLEMEN,
IN THE LITTLE MOMENT
THAT REMAINS to US
BETWEEN THE CRISIS,
And the CATASTROPHE,
WE MAY AS WELL
DRINK a GLASS
of CHAMPAGNE.

Paul Claudel